Beginner

Clover Series

AMBITIONS

VELC 研究会教材開発グループ

VELC Materials Development Group

Tetsuhito Shizuka   Masamichi Mochizuki   Takaaki Kumazawa

KINSEIDO

Kinseido Publishing Co., Ltd.

3-21 Kanda Jimbo-cho, Chiyoda-ku,
Tokyo 101-0051, Japan

First published in 2021 by Kinseido Publishing Co., Ltd.

Acknowlegdments

Text   Units 1 – 15   Ayed Hasian

Cover design   sein
Text design   Yasuharu Yuki
Illustrations   Hayato Kamoshita

🎧 音声ファイル無料ダウンロード

http://www.kinsei-do.co.jp/download/4119

この教科書で 🎧 DL 00 の表示がある箇所の音声は、上記 URL または QR コードにて
無料でダウンロードできます。自習用音声としてご活用ください。

- ▶ PC からのダウンロードをお勧めします。スマートフォンなどでダウンロードされる場合は、
  ダウンロード前に「解凍アプリ」をインストールしてください。
- ▶ URL は、**検索ボックスではなくアドレスバー (URL 表示欄)** に入力してください。
- ▶ お使いのネットワーク環境によっては、ダウンロードできない場合があります。

◎ CD 00   左記の表示がある箇所の音声は、教室用 CD（Class Audio CD）に収録されています。

は　し　が　き

VELC Test® （ベルクテスト）から見えてきたこと

　私たち VELC 研究会は，VELC Test® という日本人大学生の総合的英語熟達度をリスニング面とリーディング面から推定する標準テストを開発し，実施・運営をしているグループです。VELC Test® は 2013 年度より全国各地の多くの大学生のみなさんに受験していただいています。

　私たちは毎年，大学名や個人名が削除された解答データを分析し，テストの信頼性・妥当性をチェックしつつ，多くの受験者に共通して見られる学力プロファイル（リスニング，リーディングのスキル別の熟達度パターン）を調べています。その中から，日本人大学生にはどのような点で「伸びしろ」があるのか，どのような点を補強すればさらに英語力が伸びるのかについて，次のようなヒントを得ました。

〈リスニング〉

　まず単語レベルですが，自己流の発音ではなく英語母語話者の発音イメージで単語を記憶しておくことが大切です。そうでない人は，目で見た場合の語彙力と耳で聞いた場合の語彙力がアンバランスなものになります。

　次に目で見た場合の英文と耳で聞いた場合の英文のイメージのギャップを埋めることです。書いてある英文では，単語の切れ目はスペースによってわかり，すべての単語がはっきりとした黒い文字で印刷してあります。しかし，リスニングでは機能語が弱く発音されたり，語と語がつながって発音されたりと，書いてある英文とはかなり異なったイメージになります。そのような現実の音声に慣れておくことが必要なのです。

〈リーディング〉

　単語レベルでは何といっても語彙のサイズを増やすことが大切です。一瞬見ただけで意味が想起できるようになっている単語を増やしておくことが，リーディング力の基礎となります。

　次に文構造を見抜く力です。リスニングに比べて一つの文が長くなる傾向にあるリーディングにおいては文法力が重要になります。なんとなく単語の意味をつなげて文の意味をとろうとせず，主語と述語の対応や，修飾語句の範囲などを常にきちんと押さえながら，厳密に意味をとろうとする姿勢が大切です。

　また，文レベルの明示的な意味を理解することに加えて，その理解をもとに文と文のつながりをつかみ，テキスト全体の大意を読み取り，さらに暗示的なニュアンスまでも読み取ることが重要です。

〈リスニング＆リーディング〉

　最後にどちらにも共通するのは，その時点までに理解した内容から，次の部分を予測しながら進んでゆくという姿勢です。これまでの内容をさらに詳しく説明する内容が来そうか，対立する論点が出されそうか，あるいは話題が転換しそうなのか，などを常に考えながら聞く，また読む習慣が必要なのです。

このような現状分析を踏まえ，日本人大学生のみなさんが，自分たちの弱点を克服し，総合的な英語力をさらに伸ばしてもらえるレベル別のコースブックを作りたい，という私たちの思いを形にしたのが，この **AMBITIONS** シリーズです。

レベルの設定

この **Beginner**（入門）レベルでは，高校までで学んだ事柄を再確認しながら大学生としての英語力の基礎を身につけることを目標としています。リスニングのダイアログとリーディングの英文は，日本人大学生のための標準的な単語リスト『新 JACET8000』の 1,000 ～ 2,000 語レベルで 8 割以上をカバーしています。

テーマと英文素材

題材のテーマは「異文化理解」「食」「外国語学習」「スポーツ」「ファッション」「生物」「芸術」「グローバル・イシュー」「日本文化」「人権」「健康・医療」「環境問題」「経済・産業」「法律」「サイエンス＆テクノロジー」と多岐にわたっています。現代に生きるみなさんにぜひ知っておいていただきたい事実や問題意識を深めていただきたい事柄を厳選しました。文系のみなさんにも理系のみなさんにも興味をもって取り組んでいただけます。

素材はすべてネイティブスピーカーが，みなさんに適したレベルの語彙と表現を用いてあらたに書き下ろしました。各ユニットのテーマにまつわる取り組みやすい対話文と，そのテーマをさらに発展させた形のエッセイが組み合わさっています。1 つのテーマについて聞き，さらに読み，それについて簡単な英語で言ってみる，書いてみる，という体験ができます。

ユニットの構成

1 つの Unit は LISTENING PART と READING PART からなっています。さらに詳しくどのような構成になっているかは「使い方のヒント」に述べますが，リスニングに関してもリーディングに関しても単に内容の理解にとどまらず，使われている表現を自分で言ってみる／書いてみる，ならびに題材に対する自分の意見を言ってみる／書いてみるという活動ができる構成となっているのが本書の特長です。積極的にスピーキングとライティングにも取り組むことで，4 技能を統合的に伸ばすことができるでしょう。

本書を使うことでみなさんが英語運用能力のみならず，情報を収集し，批判的に考え，自分の考えをまとめて発表する力を伸ばしてくださることが私たちの望みです。

最後になりましたが，英文テキストを作成いただいた Ayed Hasian 先生に，心より御礼を申し上げます。

著者一同

使い方のヒント

LISTENING PART

Listen In

　音声録音されたダイアログ（対話）について，聞き取るべきポイントが日本語で用意されています。イラストをヒントにしつつ，その答えを見つけるつもりで焦点を絞って聞きましょう。

Check the Points

　ダイアログの内容についての３つの質問があり，その答えを選ぶ活動です。**Listen In** でのヒントに関連する内容が問われていますので，まず正確に聞き取りましょう。質問は英語で理解できるようにし，わからない場合には日本語を参考にしましょう。

Check the Details

　ダイアログの英文が印刷されており，５箇所に空所が設けてあります。もう一度今度はこの英文を見ながらダイアログを聞き，空所に入る語を書き取りましょう。各空所には，頭文字がヒントとして与えられています。正解を確認したら，最後にもう一度英文を見ずにダイアログ全体を聞き，すべての語句が聞き取れるまで，何度も聞き直しましょう。

Listening Focus + Practice

　リスニングに上達するためのヒントが解説してあります。読んで理解した上で，音声を聞き，説明されている現象を確認しましょう。つぎに *Practice* で，ダイアログとは別の英文を用いてさらに *Listening Focus* について理解を深めましょう。

さらに…

- **Check the Points** の質問と答えを，相手とアイコンタクトをとりながら言えるまで，ペアで練習しましょう。
- **Check the Details** で空所が埋まったスクリプトを見ながら，登場人物になったつもりでペアで読み合う練習をしましょう。最終的には英文を見ずにダイアログがおおよそ再現できるまで何度も練習しましょう。

READING PART

Find Out

　メインとなるリーディングの素材です。最初は，知らない単語があったとしても辞書を使わず，おおよその意味を前後の文脈から推測しながら，最後まで読みましょう。難しい語句や固有名詞は **Notes** に説明してありますので参照してください。

　次に録音音声を聞きながら英文を目で追う形で読んでください。音声のイントネーションや切れ目が，英文の文法構造のヒントになることもあります。

　最後に確認として，知らない単語を辞書で調べながら精読してみましょう。

Check the Points

　リーディング素材の内容に関して，リスニングによる空所補充と内容真偽を組み合わせたものです。まず音声を聞いて，読まれた方を選び，その上で，True か False かを判定しましょう。

Reading Focus + Practice

　リーディングに上達するためのヒントが解説してあります。よく読んで，*Practice* をやってみましょう。

Practice More

　Reading Focus で学習した事項を用いて英文を作り出す練習です。日本語訳と頭文字のヒントを参考にして下線部を完成してください。

Say What You Think

　リーディング素材に書いてあった事柄について，自分の意見を考えるようになるための練習です。3つの英文が準備してありますので，日本語のヒントも参考にして，自分の意見と同じまたは近いほうのいずれかを選び，自分の意見を言ってみましょう。

さらに…

- メインのリーディング素材は，意味が分かってからも繰り返し，なるべく速く黙読する練習をしてください（repeated reading と言います）。語彙の認識スピードを速くするよいトレーニングになります。
- *Say What You Think* を用いて，ペアで意見を言い合う形でスピーキング練習をしましょう。また自分の意見をまとめて 30 語くらいで書いてみましょう。

Table of Contents

Unit	Theme	Listening Part	
		Listening Focus	**Reading Focus**
1	**Cross-Cultural Understanding**	強く発音される語を聞き取る	文の主語を見つける
2	**Foods**	似た音に注意する（1） L と R	文の動詞を見つける
3	**Foreign Language Learning**	似た音に注意する（2） 2種類の「ア」	動詞の目的語を見つける
4	**Sports**	似た音に注意する（3） 子音の直後に来る L と R	補語を見つける
5	**Fashion**	弱い助動詞を聞き取る	何の代わりかを見抜く （代名詞）
6	**Living Things**	イントネーションに注意して聞く	「to ＋ 動詞」を理解する （不定詞）
7	**Art**	似た音に注意する（4） B と V	「動詞 ＋ ing」を理解する （動名詞）
8	**Global Issues**	弱い前置詞を聞き取る	主語が「されること」 を理解する（受動態）
9	**Japanese Culture**	消える d を聞き取る	比較を理解する （比較級・最上級）
10	**Human Rights**	消える t を聞き取る	後ろからの説明を見抜く （後置修飾）
11	**Health & Medical Issues**	似た音に注意する（5） TH と S	名詞を限定していることを見抜く（関係代名詞）
12	**Environmental Issues**	t でつながる語句を聞き取る	and がつなぐものを見抜く（並列1）
13	**Economy & Industry**	n でつながる語句を聞き取る	but や or がつなぐものを見抜く（並列2）
14	**Legal Issues**	話し手の気持ちを聞き取る	文脈に合った意味を選ぶ （多義語）
15	**Science & Technology**	対比による強調を理解する	知らない単語の意味を推測する

Unit 1

Cross-Cultural Understanding

☑ **Listening Focus** ➡ 強く発音される語を聞き取る
☑ **Reading Focus** ➡ 文の主語を見つける

LISTENING PART

 Listen In

 DL 02 CD1-02

アメリカ留学中のリナがアダムに，自分のしてしまったある失敗について話しています。上の
イラストを見ながら，何を失敗してしまったのか聞き取ってみましょう。

Check the Points

 DL 03 CD1-03

会話の内容に関する質問を音声で聞き，正しい答えを a ～ c から選びましょう。

1. Where was Rina?（リナはどこにいた？）
   a. At school   **b.** At home   **c.** At a restaurant

2. What was on the table?（テーブルの上に何があった？）
   a. A bag   **b.** Money   **c.** A phone

3. What did Rina do with it?（リナはそれをどうした？）
   a. She didn't touch it.   **b.** She tried to return it.
   c. She took it to the police.

Check the Details

もう一度会話を聞き，頭文字をヒントにして空所にあてはまる語を書き入れましょう。

Adam: Hi, Rina. Nana said that you had an interesting day yesterday.

Rina: Yeah, we were in a restaurant. Someone next to us forgot their
1.(**m**   ). It was on the table when they left.

Adam: Uh-oh. I hope you didn't 2.(**t**   ) it.

Rina: Actually, I picked up the money and tried to 3.(**r**   ) it to
them.

Adam: Haha. Well, that's an honest 4.(**m**   ).

Rina: I didn't know it was the 5.(**t**   ). I was so embarrassed.

Listening Focus

■ 強く発音される語を聞き取る

　英語には強く発音される語と弱く発音される語があります。名詞，動詞，形容詞，副詞などが強く発音される語の仲間です。これらの語さえ聞き取れば，かなりの程度の意味をつかむことができます。

⇨ It was on the table when they left. では，
　...... table ...... left. だけで，かなりの意味がわかります。

⇨ Actually, I picked up the money ... では，
　Actually, ... picked up ...... money だけで，おおよその意味がわかります。

　リスニングではすべての語が聞こえないことも多いので，よく聞こえた語だけから，できる限り意味をつかもうとする姿勢も大切です。

Practice

次の英文を聞き，（　）内で指定された数の強く読まれている語に下線を引きましょう。引いたら，強く読まれている語を意識しながら，真似をして言ってみましょう。

1. I'm glad you liked it.（2語）

2. She wasn't surprised at all.（3語）

3. Raise your hand if you know the answer.（4語）

READING PART

 Find Out

 DL 07 — CD1-07

次のエッセイを読み，設問に答えましょう。

A Noisy Neighbor

Do you have a noisy neighbor? People solve this problem in different ways. In some cultures, people talk to the building manager when their neighbors make too
5 much noise. They do not want to talk to their neighbors face to face. In other places, people are more comfortable talking directly to their neighbors. They
don't want to add more people to the problem. To solve a problem, do you prefer
10 to communicate directly or indirectly? Solutions may differ from person to person and from culture to culture.

Notes

neighbor「隣人」 **directly**「直接」 **prefer**「〜のほうを好む」

Check the Points

DL 08 — CD1-08

音声を聞き，太字の語句のどちらが用いられているかを選びましょう。音声は2回繰り返されます。そして，完成した英文が本文の内容と合っていれば T (True) を，合っていなければ F (False) を選びましょう。

1. People solve the noisy-neighbor problem [**differently** / **similarly**]. **[T / F]**

2. Some people complain to their noisy neighbors [**directly** / **using gestures**].
[T / F]

■ 文の主語を見つける

次の英文の太字部分はその文の主語です。

1. **I** live in an apartment. (私はアパートに住んでいます)
2. Do **you** cook? (あなたは料理をしますか)
3. **Most students** have some kind of part-time job.
   (ほとんどの学生は何かしらのバイトをしています)

主語とは，「誰が（は）」「何が（は）」にあたる部分です。文の最初のほうにあることが多いですが，疑問文の場合には位置が変わるので注意しましょう。

Practice

次の英文の主語に下線を引きましょう。

1. In some cultures, people talk to the building manager.

2. To solve a problem, do you prefer to communicate directly?

3. Solutions may differ from person to person.

Practice More

次の英文の下線部には主語が入ります。日本語訳と頭文字のヒントを参考にして，文を完成させましょう。

1. 一部の生徒は高校でフランス語を学習します。

   S＿＿＿＿＿＿ s＿＿＿＿＿＿ study French at high school.

2. 私の姉（妹）はインスタグラムでフォロワーがたくさんいます。

   M＿＿＿＿＿＿ s＿＿＿＿＿＿ has a lot of followers on Instagram.

3. あの背の高い男の人は誰ですか。

   Who is that t＿＿＿＿＿＿ m＿＿＿＿＿＿?

🎧 *Say What You Think*

DL 09   CD1-09

日本語のヒントを参考にして次の文を読み，自らの意見に合うように表現を〔　　〕内から選びましょう。選んだら，その文を自分の意見として言ってみましょう。

1. I [**think** / **don't think**] many Japanese are shy.
（私は日本人の多くが内気だと思う／思わない）

2. I [**enjoy** / **don't enjoy**] talking to my neighbors.
（私は隣人と話すのを楽しむ／楽しまない）

3. I [**think** / **don't think**] it is better to communicate directly.
（私は人と直接コミュニケーションをとるほうがよいと思う／思わない）

Unit 2
Foods

☑ **Listening Focus** ⇒ 似た音に注意する（1）LとR
☑ **Reading Focus** ⇒ 文の動詞を見つける

LISTENING PART

 **Listen In**　　　　　　　　　　　　🎧 DL 10　◎ CD1-10

ティムとサクラが今夜何を食べるかについて話しています。上のイラストを見ながら，何を注文することになりそうか聞き取ってみましょう。

 **Check the Points**　　　　　　　🎧 DL 11　◎ CD1-11

会話の内容に関する質問を音声で聞き，正しい答えを a〜c から選びましょう。

1. What does Tim suggest for dinner?（ティムが夕食に提案したのは？）
　　a. Pizza　　　**b.** Pasta　　　**c.** Tacos

2. What is Tim's favorite?（ティムの一番好きなものは？）
　　a. Fruit cake　　　**b.** Pineapple pizza　　　**c.** Beef tacos

3. Will Sakura try Tim's favorite?（サクラはティムの好みのものを食べてみる？）
　　a. Yes.　　　**b.** No.　　　**c.** We don't know.

Check the Details

もう一度会話を聞き，頭文字をヒントにして空所にあてはまる語を書き入れましょう。

Tim: I'm getting hungry. How about ¹·(**p**   ) for dinner?

Sakura: Sure. Pizza sounds good. What kind of pizza do you want?

Tim: Let's get a pineapple pizza. It's my ²·(**f**   ).

Sakura: What? You're joking, right? You put ³·(**f**   ) on a pizza?

Tim: I'm ⁴·(**s**   ). It's delicious. You have to try it.

Sakura: Okay. I will. But let's order a ⁵·(**n**   ) pizza too… just in case.

Listening Focus

DL 13 CD1-13

■ 似た音に注意する（1）L と R

英語には日本語にない音があり，それらの音が他の音と聞き分けられるようになることが大切です。この Unit では L と R の音の区別に注意しましょう。

⇨ You're joking, right?
この right は「正しい」という意味の語ですが，L を用いた light であれば「光」などを意味する別の語になります。

L は舌先をしっかり歯ぐきあるいは歯の裏につけて発音されます。R は舌先をどこにもつけずに発音されます。

Practice

DL 14 CD1-14

次の英文を聞き，[ ] 内で言われているほうの語に○をつけましょう。音声を聞き確認したら，真似をして言ってみましょう。

1. She is a good [**leader** / **reader**]. ▶ leader「指導者」 reader「読者」
2. She is a good [**leader** / **reader**].
3. That's your [**light** / **right**]. ▶ light「明かり」 right「権利」
4. That's your [**light** / **right**].

 Find Out

🎧 DL 15　◎ CD1-15

次のエッセイを読み，設問に答えましょう。

Why Coffee Is Good for You

　　Do you enjoy your morning coffee? Coffee is not just a popular drink. It can help you in your daily life. First, coffee makes your body burn fat more
5　quickly. Many people drink coffee every day because they want to lose weight. Second, it can help you stay awake. Students often drink coffee during long classes. In addition, coffee can help protect you from some diseases. This means
10　that coffee drinkers are living longer lives. However, you should not drink more than three or four cups a day.

Notes

burn fat「脂肪を燃やす」　**stay awake**「起きている」

Check the Points

🎧 DL 16　◎ CD1-16

音声を聞き，太字の語句のどちらが用いられているかを選びましょう。音声は2回繰り返されます。そして，完成した英文が本文の内容と合っていれば T (True) を，合っていなければ F (False) を選びましょう。

1. Some people drink coffee to [**gain** / **lose**] weight.　　　　**[T / F]**

2. Drinking [**ten** / **three**] cups of coffee every day is okay.　　**[T / F]**

Reading Focus

■ **文の動詞を見つける**
　次の英文の太字部分をその文の動詞と言います。

1. I **am** a university student.（私は大学生です）
2. We **come** to this campus by bus.（私たちはこのキャンパスにバスで来ます）
3. Ken can **play** tennis very well.（ケンはテニスをとても上手にプレーできます）

　動詞は，主語の状態や動作を表します。1 の am は be 動詞と言い，主語の状態を表します。2 の come は一般動詞で，主語の動作を表します。3 では一般動詞 play の前に助動詞 can が使われています。助動詞は動詞に意味を付け加えます。

Practice

次の英文の動詞に下線を引きましょう。

1. Coffee is not just a popular drink.

2. Students often drink coffee.

3. Coffee can protect you from diseases.

Practice More

次の英文の下線部には動詞などが入ります。日本語訳と頭文字のヒントを参考にして，文を完成させましょう。

1. レイと私は大学のアカペラサークルに入っています。

   Ray and I **a**＿＿＿＿＿＿＿ in the a cappella circle at university.

2 大学生は自分の時間割を作ることができます。

   University students **c**＿＿＿＿＿＿ **m**＿＿＿＿＿＿ their own class schedule.

3. 私たちのクラスのほとんどの学生は一人暮らしです。

   Most students in our class **l**＿＿＿＿＿＿ alone.

Say What You Think

日本語のヒントを参考にして次の文を読み，自らの意見に合うように表現を［　　］内から選びましょう。選んだら，その文を自分の意見として言ってみましょう。

1. I [**think / don't think**] drinking coffee is good for our health.
   （コーヒーを飲むのは健康にいいと思う／思わない）

2. I [**think / don't think**] doing exercise is healthier than drinking coffee.
   （運動をするほうがコーヒーを飲むより健康的だと思う／思わない）

3. I prefer [**coffee to tea / tea to coffee**].
   （私は紅茶よりコーヒーが／コーヒーより紅茶が好きだ）

Unit 3

Foreign Language Learning

☑ **Listening Focus** ⇒ 似た音に注意する（2）2種類の「ア」
☑ **Reading Focus** ⇒ 動詞の目的語を見つける

LISTENING PART

 **Listen In** 🎧DL 18 💿CD1-18

ユカリがダンに今日のできごとを伝えています。上のイラストを見ながら，ユカリがどんな体験をしたのか聞き取ってみましょう。

 **Check the Points** 🎧DL 19 💿CD1-19

会話の内容に関する質問を音声で聞き，正しい答えをa〜cから選びましょう。

1. Who did Yukari meet today?（ユカリは今日誰に会った？）
   a. Tourists from Australia   **b.** Tourists from America
   c. Tourists from Canada

2. What did they ask Yukari for?（彼らはユカリに何を求めた？）
   a. Directions   **b.** Help with their bags   **c.** Money

3. How long was Yukari with them?（ユカリは彼らとどのくらい一緒にいた？）
   a. About 30 seconds   **b.** A couple of minutes   **c.** Several hours

⌕ *Check the Details*

🎧 DL 20　◎ CD1-20

もう一度会話を聞き，頭文字をヒントにして空所にあてはまる語を書き入れましょう。

Yukari: Guess what! I met some nice ^{1.}(**t**) from Canada today.

Dan: That's great. Were they able to ^{2.}(**s**) Japanese?

Yukari: No. We spoke in English. They ^{3.}(**a**) me for directions.

Dan: You are so kind! Good job.

Yukari: It was ^{4.}(**f**) for me too. Actually, I walked around Osaka with them all afternoon.

Dan: Wow! You can be a professional tour ^{5.}(**g**)!

Listening Focus

🎧 DL 21　◎ CD1-21

■ 似た音に注意する（2） 2種類の「ア」

この Unit では日本語の「ア」に近い2種類の音に注意しましょう。

⇨ I met some nice tourists.
　　some をはっきり発音すると /sʌm/ です。カタカナでは同じ「サム」でも，Sam（サム：男子の名）は /sæm/ と発音されます。

⇨ It was fun for me too.
　　この fun /fʌn/ は「楽しみ」という意味の語ですが，fan /fæn/ であれば「愛好者，ファン」という意味の別の語になります。

Practice

🎧 DL 22　◎ CD1-22

次の英文を聞き，[　　]内で言われているほうの語に○をつけましょう。音声を聞き確認したら，真似をして言ってみましょう。

1. Don't touch the [**bug** / **bag**].　　▶ bug「虫」 bag「カバン」
2. Don't touch the [**bug** / **bag**].
3. I saw a [**hut** / **hat**] there.　　▶ hut「小屋」 hat「帽子」
4. I saw a [**hut** / **hat**] there.

12

READING PART

 **Find Out**

DL 23 CD1-23

次のエッセイを読み，設問に答えましょう。

Benefits of Studying with Music

    Do you enjoy studying English? Do you like music too? If you do, studying with English music is perfect for you. Naturally, English songs can improve
5 your listening. You can hear natural English every day. Also, you can learn new words and grammar from the lyrics. Write down new phrases and check their meaning online. Finally, singing is good for your speaking. Every time you sing a
10 song, you are practicing pronunciation. Studying with music is a great way to learn and have fun as well!

Notes

naturally「当然ながら」 **improve**「上達させる」 **lyrics**「歌詞」 **pronunciation**「発音」

 **Check the Points**

DL 24 CD1-24

音声を聞き，太字の語句のどちらが用いられているかを選びましょう。音声は２回繰り返されます。そして，完成した英文が本文の内容と合っていれば T (True) を，合っていなければ F (False) を選びましょう。

1. If you like English and music, you [**should** / **should not**] study with English songs.   **[T / F]**

2. Singing English songs [**is** / **is not**] good for practicing pronunciation.   **[T / F]**

Reading Focus

■ **動詞の目的語を見つける**

次の英文の下線部は動詞で，太字部分はその目的語です。

1. I <u>love</u> **pizza**. (私はピザが大好きです)
2. They <u>play</u> **basketball** on weekends. (彼らは週末にバスケットボールをします)
3. Music <u>makes</u> **us** happy. (音楽は私たちをハッピーにします)

目的語とは，動詞の動作の対象となる部分のことです。

Practice

次の英文の下線部の動詞の目的語を四角で囲みましょう。

1. Do you <u>enjoy</u> studying English?

2. I <u>learn</u> new words from the lyrics.

3. Every time you <u>sing</u> a song, you <u>are practicing</u> pronunciation.

Practice More

次の英文の空所には目的語が入ります。日本語訳と頭文字のヒントを参考にして，文を完成させましょう。

1. 私は何か温かいものが飲みたいです。

I want to drink **s**_____ hot.

2. 自分の昼食を持参してください。

Please bring your own **l**_____.

3. 彼女は毎日たくさんの写真を撮ります。

She takes a lot of **p**_____ every day.

🅰 *Say What You Think*

 DL 25 ⊙ CD1-25

日本語のヒントを参考にして次の文を読み，自らの意見に合うように表現を［　　］内から選びましょう。選んだら，その文を自分の意見として言ってみましょう。

1. I [**think / don't think**] it is fun to sing karaoke.
（カラオケを歌うのは楽しいと思う／思わない）

2. I [**like / don't like**] singing songs in English.
（私は英語の歌を歌うのが好きだ／好きでない）

3. I [**think / don't think**] we need to understand the lyrics when we sing an English song.
（英語の歌を歌うときは歌詞を理解する必要があると思う／思わない）

Sports

> ☑ **Listening Focus** ⇨ 似た音に注意する（3）
> 子音の直後に来る L と R
> ☑ **Reading Focus** ⇨ 補語を見つける

LISTENING PART

Listen In
DL 26　CD1-26

リョウがアンナを誘ってプロ野球の試合観戦に来ています。上のイラストを見ながら、日本の
プロ野球とアメリカ・メジャーリーグの試合の違いを聞き取ってみましょう。

Check the Points
DL 27　CD1-27

会話の内容に関する質問を音声で聞き、正しい答えを a ～ c から選びましょう。

1. How many times did Anna go to baseball games in the US?
　（アンナはアメリカで野球の試合に何度行った？）

　　a. Never　　　**b.** A few times　　　**c.** Many times

2. According to Anna, who is more energetic?（アンナによれば、誰がもっと元気？）

　　a. The Japanese crowd　　　**b.** The American crowd
　　c. The Japanese team

3. What does Anna say the Japanese crowd is doing?
　（アンナは、日本の観客が何をしていると言っている？）

　　a. Singing　　　**b.** Dancing　　　**c.** Eating

⊝ *Check the Details*

もう一度会話を聞き，頭文字をヒントにして空所にあてはまる語を書き入れましょう。

Anna: Thanks for taking me out today. This is so great.

Ryo: I'm glad you ^{1.}(**c**). Did you go to many baseball games in the US?

Anna: ^{2.}(**N**) really. I went a few times, but they weren't as fun as this!

Ryo: How were they ^{3.}(**d**)?

Anna: Well, the crowd here has much more ^{4.}(**e**)! And everyone is singing! I love it!

Ryo: I'm glad you are having fun. Oh, here comes my favorite ^{5.}(**p**)!

Listening Focus

■ 似た音に注意する（3）子音の直後に来るＬとＲ

ＬとＲの音の区別は Unit 2 でも学習しましたが，この Unit では，他の子音の直後に来るＬとＲに注意しましょう。

⇨ I'm glad you came. では，
glad は g のあとにＬが来ていますが，g のあとをＲの音で発音すると，grad（卒業生）という別の単語に聞こえます。

⇨ The crowd here ... では，
crowd は c のあとにＲが来ていますが，c のあとをＬの音で発音すると，cloud（雲）という別の単語に聞こえます。

Practice

DL 30 ⊙ CD1-30

次の英文を聞き，[ ] 内で言われているほうの語に○をつけましょう。音声を聞き確認したら，真似をして言ってみましょう。

1. I saw a big [**cloud / crowd**].

2. I saw a big [**cloud / crowd**].

3. I don't like [**flies / fries**].　　　　▶ flies「ハエ」 fries「フライドポテト」

4. I don't like [**flies / fries**].

 Find Out

🎧 DL 31　◎ CD1-31

次のエッセイを読み，設問に答えましょう。

The Origin of Soccer

　　Did you know that football is over 2,000 years old?
Some people believe that football started in England.
Ancient football players kicked balls of animal skin,
stuffed animal organs, or even human skulls! At that
5　time, the game had no rules. It was very violent. Of
course, the game has changed in many ways since
then. Some children carried and ran with the ball.
This style became the sport known as rugby. In 1863,
England created a football association that added
10　new rules, such as "no hands." This style of football
became the sport known as soccer.

Notes

ancient「古代の」　**stuffed**「詰め物をした」　**organ**「臓器」　**skull**「頭蓋骨」　**association**「協会」

 Check the Points

🎧 DL 32　◎ CD1-32

音声を聞き，太字の語句のどちらが用いられているかを選びましょう。音声は2回繰り返され
ます。そして，完成した英文が本文の内容と合っていればT（True）を，合っていなければF
（False）を選びましょう。

1. In the old days, football games [**were** / **were not**] very violent.　　　**[T / F]**

2. Football has [**changed in many ways** / **not changed at all**].　　　**[T / F]**

Reading Focus

■ 補語を見つける

次の英文の太字部分は，その文中の補語です。

1. Our teacher is **a karate champion**. （私たちの先生は空手のチャンピオンです）

2. My brother became **famous** as a YouTuber. （私の弟（兄）はユーチューバーとして有名になりました）

3. That will make my mother **happy**. （それは私の母を幸せにするでしょう）

補語とは，主語または目的語を説明する，または補う部分のことです。上の例文では，our teacher = a karate champion, my brother = famous, my mother = happy という関係があります。

Practice

次の英文の補語に下線を引きましょう。

1. Football is over 2,000 years old.

2. The game was very violent.

3. This style of football became the sport known as soccer.

Practice More

次の英文の下線部には補語（または補語の一部）が入ります。日本語訳と頭文字のヒントを参考にして，文を完成させましょう。

1. トムは高校時代からの友人です。

Tom is a **f**_____ **f**_____ high school.

2. 彼女はケンがいると嬉しそうです。

She looks **h**_____ when Ken is around.

3. あなたの最初の小説を読んでファンになりました。

I became **y**_____ **f**_____ when I read your first novel.

✏ *Say What You Think*

日本語のヒントを参考にして次の文を読み，自らの意見に合うように表現を［　　］内から選びましょう。選んだら，その文を自分の意見として言ってみましょう。

1. I [**enjoy / don't enjoy**] watching soccer games.
　（サッカーの試合を見るのが好きだ／好きではない）

2. I prefer watching [**soccer to watching rugby / rugby to watching soccer**].
　（ラグビーよりサッカー／サッカーよりラグビーを見るのが好きだ）

3. I am [**happy / not particularly happy**] that rugby is getting popular in Japan.
　（日本でラグビーの人気が上がって嬉しい／特に嬉しくはない）

Unit 5

Fashion

LISTENING PART

Listen In

 DL 34 ◎ CD1-34

マサキの買い物にジェニーがつきあっています。上のイラストを見ながら，2人が服を買うときにどのような点を重視しているかについて聞き取ってみましょう。

Check the Points

 DL 35 ◎ CD1-35

会話の内容に関する質問を音声で聞き，正しい答えを a ～ c から選びましょう。

1. What does Jenny think about the jacket? (ジェニーはジャケットについてどう思う？)
   a. Not nice   **b.** Too cheap   **c.** Too expensive

2. What is Masaki looking for in clothes? (マサキは服に何を求めている？)
   a. Good quality   **b.** Cheaper price   **c.** Eco-friendliness

3. What kind of clothes does Jenny prefer? (ジェニーはどんな服のほうが好き？)
   a. Good-quality clothes   **b.** Cheap clothes
   c. Clothes made in Japan

Check the Details

もう一度会話を聞き，頭文字をヒントにして空所にあてはまる語を書き入れましょう。

Masaki: Hey, Jenny. Check out this jacket. Isn't it great?

Jenny: Wow! It's really nice. But I think that ¹·(**p**　　　　　　　) is too high.

Masaki: Yes, it's ²·(**e**　　　　　　　), but it's a high-quality jacket. It will ³·(**l**　　　　　　) a long time.

Jenny: Personally, I like to buy cheaper clothes because I can buy more with less money.

Masaki: You also ⁴·(**t**　　　　　　　) away more clothes every year, right?

Jenny: Of course! When the clothes get ⁵·(**o**　　　　　　), I can go shopping again!

Listening Focus

■ 弱い助動詞を聞き取る

　助動詞は，強く長めにはっきりと発音される場合と，弱くすばやく曖昧に発音される場合があります。肯定文で動詞の前に来る助動詞は弱く発音されるのが普通です。

⇨ It will last a long time. （will は弱い）　Yes, it will. （will は強い）
⇨ I can go shopping again. （can は弱い）　Yes, I can. （can は強い）

Practice

次の英文の（　　）内には弱く発音される助動詞が入ります。音声を聞き，どの助動詞が入っているか選びましょう。確認したら，真似をして言ってみましょう。

1. It (　　　　　　　) begin to rain at any time.

2. I (　　　　　　) help you.

3. I (　　　　　　) never give up.

will	can	could

READING PART

 Find Out

🎧 DL 39 💿 CD1-39

次のエッセイを読み，設問に答えましょう。

Strict Japanese School Rules

Japanese schools have many strict rules about hair color. Students must have black hair. They are not allowed to color their hair. However, this is a problem for
5 students with naturally brown hair. They are often forced to dye their hair black. In 2017, a student sued Osaka prefecture because her high school made her dye her brown hair black. The school would not let her attend classes with her natural
10 hair color. Now, many schools are promising to allow natural hair colors, but the problem still continues in many schools across Japan.

Notes

allow「許す」 **color**「色をつける」 **force**「強制する」 **dye**「染める」 **sue**「訴える」

 Check the Points

🎧 DL 40 💿 CD1-40

音声を聞き，太字の語句のどちらが用いられているかを選びましょう。音声は２回繰り返されます。そして，完成した英文が本文の内容と合っていればT（True）を，合っていなければF（False）を選びましょう。

1. Some Japanese students are forced to dye their hair [**black** / **brown**].

[T / F]

2. A [**student** / **school**] in Osaka sued Osaka prefecture in 2017. [T / F]

■ 何の代わりかを見抜く（代名詞）

次の英文の太字部分は，代名詞です。

1. **She** can use **my** PC.（彼女は私のパソコンを使って構いません）
2. **They** often eat out on weekends.（彼らは週末によく外食します）
3. Many students have part-time jobs. Some of **them** work at convenience stores.（バイトをする学生は多いです。彼らの一部はコンビニで働きます）

文中で同じ名詞を何度も繰り返すのを避けたいとき，代名詞を用いることがあります。

〈代表的な代名詞〉

	1人称	2人称	3人称
主格	I, we	you	he, she, it, they
所有格	my, our	your	his, her, its, their
目的格	me, us	you	him, her, it, them

Practice

次の英文の囲み部分を指している代名詞に下線を引きましょう。

1. Students must have black hair. They are not allowed to color their hair.

2. However, this is a problem for students with naturally brown hair. They are often forced to dye their hair black.

3. In 2017, a student sued Osaka prefecture because her high school made her dye her brown hair black.

🄪 **Practice More**

次の英文の下線部には代名詞が入ります。日本語訳を参考にして，文を完成させましょう。

1. 父は51歳ですが，ずっと若く見えます。

   My father is 51 years old, but _____ looks much younger.

2. 私は彼女に屋外で遊んで欲しいです。

   I want _____ to play outdoors.

3. 私はあなたの私生活には興味がありません。

I am not interested in _____ private life.

Say What You Think

DL 41 CD1-41

日本語のヒントを参考にして次の文を読み，自らの意見に合うように表現を［　］内から選びましょう。選んだら，その文を自分の意見として言ってみましょう。

1. I [**think / don't think**] high schools should be strict about students' hair color.
（高校は生徒の髪色について厳しくあるべきだと思う／思わない）

2. I [**think / don't think**] students have a right to dye their hair.
（生徒には髪を染める権利があると思う／思わない）

3. I [**think / don't think**] Japanese schools have too many unreasonable rules.
（日本の学校には不合理なルールが多すぎると思う／思わない）

Living Things

☑ **Listening Focus** ➡ イントネーションに注意して聞く
☑ **Reading Focus** ➡ 「to ＋ 動詞」を理解する（不定詞）

LISTENING PART

Listen In
 DL 42 ◎ CD1-42

アイコとディヴィッドがある動物について話しています。上のイラストを見ながら，どんな動物を飼っているのか聞き取ってみましょう。

Check the Points
 DL 43 ◎ CD1-43

会話の内容に関する質問を音声で聞き，正しい答えを a〜c から選びましょう。

1. What animal does David have?（ディヴィッドの飼っている動物は？）
   a. A dog　　　**b.** A cat　　　**c.** A rabbit

2. Where did David get the animal?（ディヴィッドはその動物をどこで手に入れた？）
   a. At a pet shop　　　**b.** At an animal shelter　　　**c.** On the street

3. What will David do with the animal?（ディヴィッドは動物をどうする？）
   a. Give it food　　　**b.** Walk it　　　**c.** Trim it

⟲ *Check the Details*

 DL 44 ○ CD1-44

もう一度会話を聞き，頭文字をヒントにして空所にあてはまる語を書き入れましょう。

Aiko: Oh my goodness! Did you get a new 1.(**c**   )? It's so cute!

David: Actually, I didn't get him. He 2.(**c**   ) me.

Aiko: What do you 3.(**m**   )? You didn't get him from a shelter?

David: No. He 4.(**f**   ) me home last week and decided to stay.

Aiko: So he just moved in with you? That's so funny.

David: Yup. We live together now. Oh, excuse me. My new roommate is
5.(**h**   ).

| Listening Focus |

🎧 DL 45 ○ CD1-45

■ **イントネーションに注意して聞く**

　会話では，平叙文（疑問文ではない普通の文）の語順を変えずに，文の最後の単語を尻上がりに言うだけで，相手に質問していることを表すことがあります。

⇨ **You didn't get him from a shelter?**（↗）では，
shelter を尻上がりに言うことで，Didn't you get him from a shelter? と同じ意味を表しています。

⇨ **So he just moved in with you?**（↗）では，
you を尻上がりに言うことで，So did he just move in with you? と同じ意味を表しています。

| *Practice*

🎧 DL 46 ○ CD1-46

次の英文を聞き，文字通りの平叙文として言っているのか，疑問文として言っているのかを判定しましょう。平叙文の場合はピリオド，疑問文の場合はクエスチョンマークを [　　] に書き入れましょう。音声を聞き確認したら，真似をして言ってみましょう。

1. She has a new cat [　　　]

2. I didn't say that to you [　　　]

3. So they live together now [　　　]

 Find Out

DL 47　CD1-47

次のエッセイを読み，設問に答えましょう。

Puppy Mills vs. Shelters

Are you thinking about getting a new puppy? It is fun to watch cute puppies at a pet shop. However, did you know that most pet shops get dogs from "puppy
5　mills"? These are farms which breed puppies to make money. Buying puppies at pet shops means supporting these businesses. You can save an animal's life by going to a shelter instead. There, thousands of loving animals are waiting for you
10　to take them home. Unfortunately, 80 percent of them never leave. To help our furry friends, avoid pet shops and rescue a shelter animal.

Notes

puppy「子犬」　**mill**「工場」　**shelter**「シェルター（保護施設，収容施設）」　**breed**「繁殖させる」
furry「ふわふわした」

Check the Points

DL 48　CD1-48

音声を聞き，太字の語句のどちらが用いられているかを選びましょう。音声は２回繰り返されます。そして，完成した英文が本文の内容と合っていれば T (True) を，合っていなければ F (False) を選びましょう。

1. Puppy mills breed puppies for [**money** / **charity**].　　　**[T / F]**

2. You can get an animal at a [**pet shop** / **shelter**] and save its life.　**[T / F]**

Reading Focus

■「to＋動詞」を理解する（不定詞）
次の英文の太字部分を不定詞と言います。不定詞は to＋動詞の原形から成ります。

1. My brother's dream is **to become** a pilot.（兄（弟）の夢はパイロットになることです）
2. Do you have anything **to read** on the train?（列車の中で何か読むものを持っていますか）
3. My father works hard **to support** my family.
（父は家族を支えるために一生懸命働いています）

不定詞には，「〜すること」，「〜するための」，「〜するために／〜して」などの用法があります。

Practice

次の英文の不定詞に下線を引きましょう。

1. It is fun to watch cute puppies at a pet shop.

2. These are farms which breed puppies to make money.

3. There, thousands of loving animals are waiting for you to take them home.

Practice More

次の英文の下線部には不定詞が入ります。日本語訳と頭文字のヒントを参考にして，文を完成させましょう。

1. 早起きは大切です。

It is important **t**_____ **g**_____ **u**_____ early in the morning.

2. 彼の結婚について聞き，驚きました。

I was surprised **t**_____ **h**_____ of his marriage.

3. 彼は海外留学のチャンスがあったが，日本に留まりました。

He had a chance **t**____ **s**_____ **a**_____, but stayed in Japan.

🅐 *Say What You Think*

日本語のヒントを参考にして次の文を読み，自らの意見に合うように表現を ［　　］内から選びましょう。選んだら，その文を自分の意見として言ってみましょう。

1. I [**think / don't think**] it is good to buy animals at pet shops.
  （ペットショップで動物を買うことはよいことだと思う／思わない）

2. I [**want / don't want**] to get an animal at a shelter.
  （私はシェルターで動物をもらいたい／もらいたくない）

3. I [**think / don't think**] we should ban pet shops.
  （私たちはペットショップを禁止すべきだと思う／思わない）

Unit 7

Art

☑ **Listening Focus** ⟹ 似た音に注意する（4）B と V
☑ **Reading Focus** ⟹ 「動詞＋ ing」を理解する（動名詞）

LISTENING PART

 Listen In

カオリとロブがゲームについて話しています。上のイラストを見ながら，カオリがロブに何を勧めているのか聞き取ってみましょう。

 Check the Points

会話の内容に関する質問を音声で聞き，正しい答えを a 〜 c から選びましょう。

1. What is so real about the game that Kaori is playing?
   （カオリはゲームの何が本物そっくりだと言っている？）
   a. The game sound   **b.** The story of the game   **c.** The game characters

2. What does Kaori say Rob is good at?（カオリはロブが何に優れていると言っている？）
   a. Playing games   **b.** Drawing   **c.** Acting

3. What could be a fun career for Rob?（ロブにとって楽しそうな仕事とは？）
   a. Gamer   **b.** Game writer   **c.** Game artist

⊖ *Check the Details*

もう一度会話を聞き，頭文字をヒントにして空所にあてはまる語を書き入れましょう。

Kaori: Video games are so ¹·(**a**   ) nowadays. Look at this game I

am playing. These ²·(**c**   ) almost look real!

Rob: Yeah, the artists for this game are really talented.

Kaori: Hey, you're good at ³·(**d**   ), right? Why don't you become

a game artist?

Rob: Do you think I could? I don't know if I'm good enough.

Kaori: I think your artwork is great! You should give it a ⁴·(**t**   ).

Rob: Okay. That could be a fun ⁵·(**c**   ). I'll think about it!

Listening Focus

■ 似た音に注意する（4）B と V

　この Unit では B と V の音の区別に注意しましょう。/b/ は b で書かれる，日本語にもある音で，上下の唇を閉じて発音されます。/v/ は主として v で書かれる，日本語にはない音で，下唇を上の前歯に当てて発音されます。

⇨ Why don't you become a game artist? では，
become の最初に /b/ の音があります。

⇨ Video games are so amazing nowadays. では，
video の最初に /v/ の音があります。

⇨ You should give it a try. では，
give の最後に /v/ の音があります。

Practice

🎧 DL 54　◎ CD1-54

次の英文を聞き，［　　］内で言われているほうの語に○をつけましょう。音声を聞き確認したら，真似をして言ってみましょう。

1. That's my [**vest** / **best**].　　　▶ vest「胴衣，ベスト」　best「最善」
2. That's my [**vest** / **best**].
3. I need your [**vote** / **boat**].　　▶ vote「票」　boat「ボート，船」
4. I need your [**vote** / **boat**].

READING PART

Find Out

DL 55 CD1-55

次のエッセイを読み，設問に答えましょう。

Graffiti Art

Some of the world's best art pieces come from an unusual art style: graffiti. Writing or drawing on walls in public places is almost always illegal. However, seeing amazing artwork on the sides of random city buildings is becoming more and more common. One very famous graffiti artist is Banksy. This British street artist paints clever images that have strong political and social messages. One of Banksy's artworks was recently sold at an auction for over one million pounds. Painting isn't the only interesting thing about Banksy, though. In fact, no one knows exactly who this person is.

Notes

graffiti「落書き」 **art piece**「芸術作品」 **artwork**「芸術品」 **random**「無作為の，行き当たりばったりの」 **auction**「競売，オークション」 **pound**「ポンド（イギリスの通貨単位）」

Check the Points

DL 56 CD1-56

音声を聞き，太字の語句のどちらが用いられているかを選びましょう。音声は２回繰り返されます。そして，完成した英文が本文の内容と合っていればＴ(True)を，合っていなければＦ(False)を選びましょう。

1. Seeing graffiti art in public places **[is / isn't]** becoming common. **[T / F]**

2. Banksy **[sends / receives]** strong political and social messages. **[T / F]**

■「動詞＋ing」を理解する（動名詞）

次の英文の太字部分を動名詞と言います。動名詞は動詞の ing 形をとり，名詞の働きをします。

1. **Walking** is good for your health.（歩くことはあなたの健康によいです）
2. His job is **writing** computer programs.
（彼の仕事はコンピュータプログラムを書くことです）
3. She cleans the room before **going** home.（彼女は帰宅する前に部屋を掃除します）

動名詞は文中で，主語，補語，目的語になります。

Practice

次の英文の動名詞に下線を引きましょう。

1. Writing or drawing on walls in public places is almost always illegal.

2. Seeing amazing artwork on the sides of buildings is becoming more and more common.

3. Painting isn't the only interesting thing about Banksy.

Practice More

次の英文の下線部には動名詞が入ります。日本語訳と頭文字のヒントを参考にして，文を完成させましょう。

1. 男の子は宿題を終わらせたあと公園に行きました。

The boy went to the park after **f**＿＿＿＿＿＿ his (**h**＿＿＿＿＿＿).

2. そのカップルは外国の博物館を訪れるのを楽しんでいます。

The couple enjoys **v**＿＿＿＿＿＿ (**m**＿＿＿＿＿＿) in foreign countries.

3. その国で仕事を見つけるのはたいへん難しいです。

F＿＿＿＿＿＿ a (**j**＿＿＿＿＿＿) is very difficult in that country.

✺ *Say What You Think*

🎧 DL 57　◎ CD1-57

日本語のヒントを参考にして次の文を読み，自らの意見に合うように表現を ［　　］内から選びましょう。選んだら，その文を自分の意見として言ってみましょう。

1. I [**think / don't think**] it is okay to draw and paint on public buildings.
（人々は公共の建物に絵を描いてよいと思う／思わない）

2. I [**enjoy / don't enjoy**] seeing graffiti art on walls in public places.
（私は公共の場の壁にあるグラフィティ・アートを見ることが好きだ／好きではない）

3. I [**think / don't think**] public art museums should be free.
（公共の美術館は無料であるべきだと思う／思わない）

Global Issues

☑ **Listening Focus** ⇨ 弱い前置詞を聞き取る
☑ **Reading Focus** ⇨ 主語が「されること」を理解する
　　　　　　　　　　　　（受動態）

LISTENING PART

Listen In

🎧DL 58 　◎CD1-58

マークとヒロコが SNS について話しています。上のイラストを見ながら，2人の SNS に対する考え方について聞き取ってみましょう。

Check the Points

🎧DL 59 　◎CD1-59

会話の内容に関する質問を音声で聞き，正しい答えを a 〜 c から選びましょう。

1. What did Mark apply for?（マークは何に応募した？）
   a. A job　　　**b.** A scholarship　　　**c.** A prize

2. What was Mark asked to show?（マークは何を見せるように言われた？）
   a. His student card　　　**b.** His social media pages　　　**c.** His health report

3. Does Hiroko think Mark should share his private information with the company?（ヒロコは，マークが会社と個人的な情報を共有するべきだと考えている？）
   a. Yes　　　**b.** No　　　**c.** We don't know.

⟳ *Check the Details*

もう一度会話を聞き，頭文字をヒントにして空所にあてはまる語を書き入れましょう。

Mark: I applied for a ¹·(j   ) recently, but they want access to my private social media accounts.

Hiroko: Anyone can see your social media pages, right? What's the ²·(p   )?

Mark: Mine are private! I only ³·(s   ) them with my friends and family.

Hiroko: But you don't ⁴·(u   ) anything bad, do you?

Mark: I just don't think that companies need to know about our private lives.

Hiroko: I can ⁵·(a   ) with that. But if you put something online, is it still private?

Listening Focus

■ **弱い前置詞を聞き取る**

　Unit 5 で学習した助動詞と同様に，前置詞も，強く長めにはっきりと発音される場合と，弱くすばやく曖昧に発音される場合があります。文中では弱い場合が普通です。

　　⇨ I applied <u>for</u> a job recently, but they want access <u>to</u> my private social media accounts.

　　⇨ I only share them <u>with</u> my friends and family.

　上の for, to, with はすばやく弱く発音されています。for を不必要に強く発音すると four に，to を不必要に強く発音すると two や too に聞き間違えられることもあります。

Practice

下線部の前置詞の発音に注意して英文を聞きましょう。どのくらい弱いかを確認したら，真似して言ってみましょう。

1. I waited <u>for</u> four hours.

2. Are you going <u>with</u> Wes?

3. They will stay there from one <u>to</u> two weeks.

 *Find Out*

🎧 DL 63　⊙ CD1-63

次のエッセイを読み，設問に答えましょう。

Data Privacy

The internet knows a lot about you. In fact, information about what you do, watch, and buy online is collected by many websites. Data about you is sold
5　and used to help companies understand your interests. This is why you get a lot of junk email and pop-up ads on websites. Luckily, you can protect yourself by being careful. Check the safety of smartphone apps and websites before using them.
10　Also, check your privacy settings on all of your social media accounts. Make sure that your information isn't shared without your permission. Free online services can actually take a lot from you.

Notes

junk email「迷惑メール」　**pop-up ad**「インターネット閲覧中に別ウィンドウで飛び出す広告」
luckily「幸運なことに」

 *Check the Points*

🎧 DL 64　⊙ CD1-64

音声を聞き，太字の語句のどちらが用いられているかを選びましょう。音声は２回繰り返されます。そして，完成した英文が本文の内容と合っていれば T (True) を，合っていなければ F (False) を選びましょう。

1. Companies use information about your internet use to **[buy / sell]** things you may like.　**[T / F]**

2. You **[can / can't]** protect yourself by setting your internet accounts carefully.　**[T / F]**

Reading Focus

■ 主語が「されること」を理解する（受動態）
次の英文の太字部分を受動態と言います。

1. The new virus **is spread** all over the world.
(その新しいウィルスは世界中に広められました)

2. The song **was sung** and **loved** by very young children.
(その歌はとても小さい子どもたちに歌われ愛されました)

3. Our life **has been changed** by smartphones.
(私たちの生活はスマートフォンによって変えられました)

受動態は be 動詞＋過去分詞で構成され，「～される」という意味を表します。

Practice

次の英文の受動態に下線を引きましょう。

1. Information about you is collected by many websites.

2. Data about you is sold and used to help companies understand your interests.

3. Make sure that your information isn't shared without your permission.

🎧 *Practice More*

次の英文の空所には受動態が入ります。日本語訳と頭文字のヒントを参考にして，文を完成させましょう。なお，下線部には be 動詞が入ります。

1. リチウム電池は有名な日本の科学者によって発明されました。

   Lithium batteries ＿＿＿＿＿＿＿（ **i**   ) by a famous Japanese scientist.

2. その2つのテーマパークは1か月以上閉園されています。

   The two theme parks have ＿＿＿＿＿＿＿（ **c**   ) for more than a month.

3. そのスーパーマーケットではすべての物が売り切れていました。

Everything _____ (**s**   ) out in the supermarket.

Say What You Think

DL 65   CD1-65

日本語のヒントを参考にして次の文を読み，自らの意見に合うように表現を［   ］内から選びましょう。選んだら，その文を自分の意見として言ってみましょう。

1. I [**want / don't want**] to show my social media pages to everyone.
（私は自分の SNS ページを誰にでも見せたい／見せたくない）

2. I [**think / don't think**] it is dangerous to use free online services.
（無料のオンラインサービスを使うのは危険だと思う／思わない）

3. I [**think / don't think**] I am protecting myself online.
（私はオンラインで自分を守っていると思う／思わない）

Unit 9
Japanese Culture

☑ **Listing Focus** ⇨ 消える d を聞き取る
☑ **Reading Focus** ⇨ 比較を理解する
　　　　　　　　　　　　（比較級・最上級）

LISTENING PART

 **Listen In**　　　　　　　　　　　　　　　　 🎧 DL 66　◎ CD2-01

エイコとリッキーは，リッキーが経験したことについて話しています。上のイラストを見ながら，どんな話なのか聞き取ってみましょう。

 **Check the Points**　　　　　　　　　　　　🎧 DL 67　◎ CD2-02

会話の内容に関する質問を音声で聞き，正しい答えを a ～ c から選びましょう。

1. How does Ricky look?（リッキーはどんな様子？）
   a. Angry　　　**b.** Happy　　　**c.** Sleepy

2. What does Ricky use well?（リッキーは何を上手に使う？）
   a. Tires　　　**b.** Ropes　　　**c.** Chopsticks

3. What did the stranger want to start with Ricky?
   （見知らぬ人はリッキーと何を始めたかった？）
   a. A business　　　**b.** A conversation　　　**c.** A game

⟳ Check the Details

もう一度会話を聞き，頭文字をヒントにして空所にあてはまる語を書き入れましょう。

Eiko: You look a little ¹·(**i**   ), Ricky. What's wrong?

Ricky: A ²·(**s**   ) told me I "use chopsticks so well" again today. I'm ³·(**t**   ) of hearing it.

Eiko: What's wrong with that? It's a good thing.

Ricky: Even ⁴·(**c**   ) can use chopsticks! Why do they think I can't?

Eiko: They don't think that. I'm sure they only said that to start a ⁵·(**c**   ) with you.

Ricky: Oh… I see. Thanks! You speak English so well, by the way.

Eiko: Ricky!!

Listening Focus

■ 消える d を聞き取る

ある単語が d で終わり，次に来る単語が子音で始まる場合，その d は「のみ込まれる」ように発音されることがあり，そうすると聞こえにくくなります。このような「消える d」に慣れましょう。

⇨ **A stranger told me ...** では，
told は d で終わり，次に m で始まる me が来ています。told の d は聞こえません。

⇨ **... they only said that to ...** では，
said が d で終わり，次に th で始まる that が来ています。said の d は聞こえません。

Practice

🎧 DL 70 · CD2-05

次の英文の下線部の d が聞こえないことを確認しましょう。確認したら，真似をして言ってみましょう。

1. Who <u>told</u> Ken about it?

2. I <u>ride</u> my bike to school.

3. When I <u>arrived</u> there, it was dark.

42

READING PART

 Find Out

DL 71 CD2-06

次のブログを読み，設問に答えましょう。

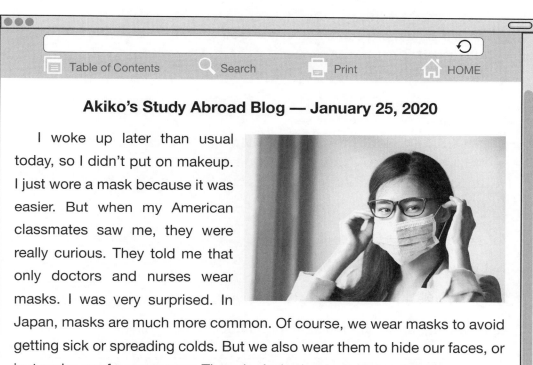

Akiko's Study Abroad Blog — January 25, 2020

I woke up later than usual today, so I didn't put on makeup. I just wore a mask because it was easier. But when my American
5 classmates saw me, they were really curious. They told me that only doctors and nurses wear masks. I was very surprised. In Japan, masks are much more common. Of course, we wear masks to avoid
10 getting sick or spreading colds. But we also wear them to hide our faces, or just make our faces warmer. They don't do that in America, I guess.

Notes

put on「身につける」 **makeup**「化粧」 **curious**「好奇心の強い」 **spread cold**「風邪を感染させる」

 Check the Points

DL 72 CD2-07

音声を聞き，太字の語句のどちらが用いられているかを選びましょう。音声は2回繰り返されます。そして，完成した英文が本文の内容と合っていれば T (True) を，合っていなければ F (False) を選びましょう。

1. Akiko wore a mask because she had [**a cold** / **no makeup on**].　　[T / F]

2. [**Americans** / **Japanese**] wear masks to make their faces warmer.　[T / F]

■ 比較を理解する（比較級・最上級）

次の英文の太字部分を比較級または最上級と言います。

1. My father left home **earlier** than usual today.
（父は今日いつもより早く家を出ました）

2. The actress is **more popular** than her sister.
（その女優は彼女の姉（妹）よりも人気があります）

3. The virus caused **the most serious** problem.
（そのウィルスはもっとも深刻な問題を引き起こしました）

比較級は形容詞や副詞の語尾に -er をつけたり，前に more をつけて，「より〜」という意味を表します。最上級は形容詞や副詞の前に the と語尾に -est をつけたり，前に the most をつけて，「もっとも〜」という意味を表します。

Practice

次の英文の比較級または最上級に下線を引きましょう。

1. I woke up later than usual today.

2. I just wore a mask because it was easier.

3. In Japan, masks are much more common.

◎ Practice More

次の英文の下線部には比較表現が入ります。日本語訳と頭文字のヒントを参考にして，文を完成させましょう。

1. 叔父は年齢より老けて見えます。

My uncle looks **o** ＿＿＿＿＿＿＿ **t** ＿＿＿＿＿＿＿ his age.

2. 地球温暖化の影響でどんどん暖かくなっています。

It is getting **w** ＿＿＿＿＿＿＿ and **w** ＿＿＿＿＿＿＿ because of global warming.

3. その男の子はもっとも難しい数学の問題を解こうとしました。

The boy tried to solve the **m** _____ **d** _____ math problem.

Say What You Think

🎧 DL 73 💿 CD2-08

日本語のヒントを参考にして次の文を読み，自らの意見に合うように表現を [　　] 内から選びましょう。選んだら，その文を自分の意見として言ってみましょう。

1. I [**think / don't think**] wearing a mask is a kind of fashion.
　　（マスクをするのは一種のファッションだと思う／思わない）

2. I [**want / don't want**] to wear a mask in summer.
　　（私は夏にマスクをつけたい／つけたくない）

3. I [**think / don't think**] people should wear a mask to protect themselves.
　　（人々は自分を守るためにマスクをすべきだと思う／思わない）

Human Rights

☑ **Listening Focus** ⇒ 消える t を聞き取る
☑ **Reading Focus** ⇒ 後ろからの説明を見抜く（後置修飾）

LISTENING PART

 **Listen In** 🎧 DL 74 💿 CD2-09

ケイトとリョウタが朝の会社で話しています。上のイラストを見ながら，リョウタが何に困っているのか聞き取ってみましょう。

 **Check the Points** 🎧 DL 75 💿 CD2-10

会話の内容に関する質問を音声で聞き，正しい答えを a ～ c から選びましょう。

1. Who did Ryota go drinking with?（リョウタは誰と飲みに行った？）
   a. His friend　　**b.** His brother　　**c.** His boss

2. What is Ryota's problem?（リョウタの問題は何？）
   a. Academic harassment　　**b.** Power harassment
   c. Sexual harassment

3. What will Ryota do the next time he gets invited to go drinking?
   （リョウタは飲みの誘いを次回はどうするつもり？）
   a. Accept　　**b.** Decline　　**c.** Leave early

🎧 *Check the Details*

🎧 DL 76 💿 CD2-11

もう一度会話を聞き，頭文字をヒントにして空所にあてはまる語を書き入れましょう。

Kate: You look really ¹·(**s**   ), Ryota. Did you work late last night?

Ryota: Kind of. My boss ²·(**i**   ) me to go drinking, and I couldn't say "no."

Kate: Again?! That's the third time this week. It's too much.

Ryota: I know, but I'm worried my boss will ³·(**d**   ) me if I don't go.

Kate: That would be power harassment! He can't ⁴·(**f**   ) you to go.

Ryota: Okay, okay. I'll decline next time. Just let me ⁵·(**s**   ) a little for now.

Listening Focus

🎧 DL 77 💿 CD2-12

■ 消える t を聞き取る

　Unit 9 では消える d について学習しましたが，t についても同様の現象があります。ある語が t で終わり，次に子音で始まる語が続くときに，t がのみこまれるように発音されて聞こえないことがあります。

　⇨ Did you work late last night? では，
　　　last が t で終わり，次に子音の n が来ています。t は聞こえません。

　⇨ ... if I don't go. では，
　　　don't が t で終わり，次に子音 g が来ています。t は聞こえません。

Practice

🎧 DL 78 💿 CD2-13

次の英文の下線部の t が聞こえないことを確認しましょう。確認したら，真似をして言ってみましょう。

1. Is this your <u>first</u> time here?

2. If you have any questions, <u>just</u> <u>let</u> me know.

3. Cats are active <u>at</u> night.

 **Find Out**

DL 79　CD2-14

次のエッセイを読み，設問に答えましょう。

Parental Leave

　What do working parents do when they have a new baby? Naturally, parents with newborn babies want to spend time with their children. Some countries allow
5 new mothers and fathers to take paid time off from work. This is called "maternity leave" (for mothers) and "paternity leave" (for fathers). Although this is a human right, not every country offers this time off. Countries offering the best paternity
10 leave include Sweden, Portugal, South Korea, and Japan. Estonia, Hungary, and Bulgaria have the best paid leave available to new mothers. Surprisingly, the US is one of the countries offering neither.

Notes

leave「休暇」　**newborn**「新生の」　**time off**「休暇」　**maternity**「母の」　**paternity**「父の」
surprisingly「驚くべきことに」

 **Check the Points**

DL 80　CD2-15

音声を聞き，太字の語句のどちらが用いられているかを選びましょう。音声は2回繰り返されます。そして，完成した英文が本文の内容と合っていればT (True) を，合っていなければF (False) を選びましょう。

1. Maternity leave is paid time off from work for [**fathers** / **mothers**].

[T / F]

2. New mothers receive the best paid leave in [**Bulgaria** / **the US**].　[T / F]

Reading Focus

■ 後ろからの説明を見抜く（後置修飾）
次の英文の太字部分を後置修飾と言います。後置修飾は前の名詞を修飾します。

1. The girls **practicing on the stage** belong to the dance club.
（ステージで練習している少女たちはダンスクラブに所属しています）
2. A lot of people have been saved by the medicine **invented in the 2010s**.
（多くの人が2010年代に発明された薬で救われています）
3. Everybody welcomed the plan **to extend the railroad to their village**.
（誰もが彼らの村まで鉄道を延長する計画を歓迎しました）

　1は practicing 以下が「ステージで練習している」という意味で「少女たち」を修飾しています。2は invented 以下が「2010年代に発明された」という意味で「薬」を修飾しています。3は to extend 以下が「彼らの村まで鉄道を延長する」という意味で「計画」を修飾しています。

Practice

次の英文の後置修飾に下線を引きましょう。

1. Parents with newborn babies want to spend time with their children.

2. Countries offering the best paternity leave include Sweden, Portugal, South Korea, and Japan.

3. The US is one of the countries offering neither.

Practice More

次の英文の下線部には後置修飾が入ります。日本語訳と頭文字のヒントを参考にして、文を完成させましょう。

1. あのバンドでギターを弾いている男性は誰ですか。

Who is the man **p**＿＿＿＿＿ the **g**＿＿＿＿＿ in that band?

2. 叔父は湖の近くの村に住んでいます。

My uncle lives in a village **n**_____ a **l**_____.

3. ハードディスクは父によって録画されたテレビ番組でいっぱいです。

The hard disk is full of TV programs **r**_____ by **m**_____
f_____.

 Say What You Think

🎧 DL 81　◎ CD2-16

日本語のヒントを参考にして次の文を読み，自らの意見に合うように表現を [　　] 内から選びましょう。選んだら，その文を自分の意見として言ってみましょう。

1. I [**think** / **don't think**] everyone should be given paid leave when they have babies.
（赤ちゃんが産まれたら誰もが育児休暇を与えられるべきだと思う／思わない）

2. I [**want** / **don't want**] to take parental leave when I become a parent.
（私は親になったら育児休暇を取りたい／取りたくない）

3. I [**think** / **don't think**] all countries should offer at least a three-month paid parental leave.
（すべての国は最低 3 か月の育児休暇を出すべきだと思う／思わない）

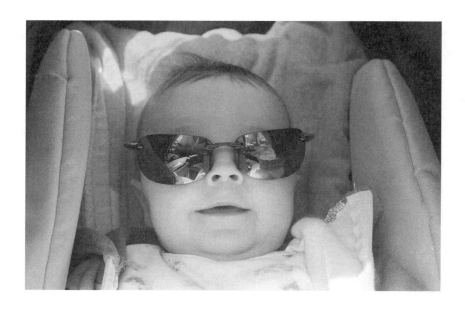

Unit 11

Health & Medical Issues

☑ **Listening Focus** ➡ 似た音に注意する（5）THとS
☑ **Reading Focus** ➡ 名詞を限定していることを見抜く
（関係代名詞）

LISTENING PART

 **Listen In**　　　　　　　　　　　　🎧 DL 82　◎ CD2-17

モエミとクリスは親知らず（wisdom teeth）について話しています。上のイラストを見ながら，モエミに何があったのか聞き取ってみましょう。

 **Check the Points**　　　　　　　🎧 DL 83　◎ CD2-18

会話の内容に関する質問を音声で聞き，正しい答えを a 〜 c から選びましょう。

1. What is wrong with Moemi's wisdom teeth? （モエミの親知らずに何があった？）
   a. They are growing straight up.　　**b.** They are growing sideways.
   c. They are not growing much.

2. How many wisdom teeth does Chris have? （クリスには親知らずが何本ある？）
   a. Two　　　**b.** Four　　　**c.** None

3. Why does Moemi say Chris is lucky?
   （モエミは，どうしてクリスが幸運だと言っている？）
   a. He has a big mouth.　　**b.** He has a big face.　　**c.** He has straight teeth.

51

⊖ **Check the Details**

もう一度会話を聞き，頭文字をヒントにして空所にあてはまる語を書き入れましょう。

Moemi: Ow ow owww. My teeth hurt. I have to have surgery to remove my
wisdom teeth.

Chris: Ouch. That's too bad. Are they not coming out ^{1.}(**s**)?

Moemi: No. They are growing sideways and ^{2.}(**p**) the other
teeth. Did that happen to you?

Chris: Nope. I still have all ^{3.}(**f**) of my wisdom teeth. See?

Moemi: Wow. Your teeth are all straight, too. You're so ^{4.}(**l**)!

Chris: I have a really big mouth, so there's ^{5.}(**p**) of room!

Listening Focus

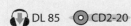

■ 似た音に注意する（5）THとS

　このUnitでは，無声のTH /θ/ の音に注意しましょう。無声のTHは舌先を歯と歯の間に挟むようにして息を出すことで発音されます。Sと似ているようですが，実はかなり異なる音です。

⇨ My teeth hurt. では，
teeth の最後に無声の TH が聞かれます。

⇨ I have a really big mouth, ... では，
mouth の最後が無声の TH です。これを S の音で発音すると mouse（マウス，ネズミ）という別の語になります。

Practice

次の単語のどちらが発音されているか聞き取りましょう。音声を聞き確認したら，真似をして言ってみましょう。

1. mouth　/　mouse
2. mouth　/　mouse
3. thing　/　sing　　　▶ thing「物」 sing「歌う」
4. thing　/　sing
5. path　/　pass　　　▶ path「小道」 pass「パスする」
6. path　/　pass

READING PART

 *Find Out*

🎧 DL 87   ◉ CD2-22

次のエッセイを読み，設問に答えましょう。

Therapy Animals

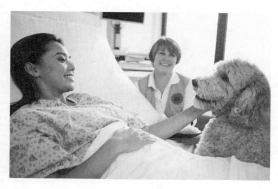

Animals support humans in various ways every day. Guide dogs help people who cannot see, and rescue dogs help find earthquake survivors. But have

5 you heard of "therapy animals"? These pets help people who are stressed out, depressed, or traumatized. They are gentle heroes that visit hospitals, nursing

homes, and even disaster areas. Therapy animals are friends to people who feel

10 lonely, and they make scared children feel safe. Dogs are not the only animals that give this kind of support, though. Sometimes cats, rabbits, and even horses work as therapy animals too.

> **Notes**
>
> **therapy**「治療のための」 **survivor**「生存者」 **depressed**「意気消沈した」
> **traumatized**「心的外傷を負った」

Check the Points

🎧 DL 88   ◉ CD2-23

音声を聞き，太字の語句のどちらが用いられているかを選びましょう。音声は２回繰り返されます。そして，完成した英文が本文の内容と合っていれば T (True) を，合っていなければ F (False) を選びましょう。

1. Therapy animals help [**animals** / **people**] in need of support.　　　**[T / F]**

2. Therapy animals include dogs, cats, and [**horses** / **pandas**].　　　**[T / F]**

■ 名詞を限定していることを見抜く（関係代名詞）

次の英文の太字部分は，その文中にある関係代名詞で，囲み部分を修飾しています。

1. Madeline is a │professor│ **who** teaches economics.
（マドリーンは経済学を教える教授です）

2. Madeline is a │professor│ **whose** father teaches philosophy.
（マドリーンは哲学を教える父がいる教授です）

関係代名詞は，名詞を後ろから修飾することができます。その名詞が人の場合，物の場合によって関係代名詞を使い分けます。また，主格，所有格，または目的格のいずれかによっても使い分けます。

	主格（〜は）	所有格（〜の）	目的格（〜を，に）
人の場合	who	whose	whom
物の場合	which	whose	which
すべて	that	------	that

Practice

次の英文の関係代名詞に下線を引き，それによって修飾されている名詞を四角で囲みましょう。

1. Guide dogs help people who cannot see, and rescue dogs help find earthquake survivors.

2. They are gentle heroes that visit hospitals, nursing homes, and even disaster areas.

3. Therapy animals are friends to people who feel lonely, and they make scared children feel safe.

4. Dogs are not the only animals that give this kind of support, though.

⚙ *Practice More*

次の英文の下線部には関係代名詞が入ります。関係代名詞 who, whose, whom, which のいずれかを用いて文を完成させましょう。

1. 私には以前、職場によく朝早く来る同僚がいました。

I once had a co-worker _____ often came early to the office in the morning.

2. 経済学は消費を研究する分野です。

Economics is a field _____ studies consumption.

3. 私はジムという名前の人とさっき話しました。

I just talked to someone _____ name was Jim.

⚙ *Say What You Think*

 DL 89 ◎ CD2-24

日本語のヒントを参考にして次の文を読み，自らの意見に合うように表現を［　　］内から選びましょう。選んだら，その文を自分の意見として言ってみましょう。

1. I [**think / don't think**] therapy rabbits can help people feel better.
（セラピーうさぎは人々の気分をよくすると思う／思わない）

2. I [**think / don't think**] nursing homes should keep therapy animals.
（老人ホームはセラピーアニマルを飼うべきだと思う／思わない）

3. I [**think / don't think**] we should stop animal testing.
（私たちは動物実験をやめるべきだと思う／思わない）

Unit 12

Environmental Issues

☑ **Listening Focus** ⟹ t でつながる語句を聞き取る
☑ **Reading Focus** ⟹ and がつなぐものを見抜く（並列 1）

LISTENING PART

 **Listen In**　　　　　　　　　　　🎧 DL 90　◎ CD2-25

ハルカとアレックスがビーチに遊びに来ています。上のイラストを見ながら，ビーチがどんな
様子なのか聞き取ってみましょう。

 **Check the Points**　　　　　🎧 DL 91　◎ CD2-26

会話の内容に関する質問を音声で聞き，正しい答えを a〜c から選びましょう。

1. How does the beach look?（ビーチはどんな様子？）
   a. Clean　　　**b.** Dirty　　　**c.** Beautiful

2. What did Haruka find in the water?（ハルカが水の中に見つけたものは？）
   a. A dead fish　　　**b.** Surfboards　　　**c.** Frisbee

3. What are Haruka and Alex likely to do?（ハルカとアレックスはこれから何をする？）
   a. Swim　　　**b.** Go home　　　**c.** Play on the beach

Check the Details
🎧 DL 92　💿 CD2-27

もう一度会話を聞き，頭文字をヒントにして空所にあてはまる語を書き入れましょう。

Haruka: Yay! The beach! I'm so excited! I can't wait to get in the wa... eww!

Alex: Aww, man. Why is the ocean brown? The water looks really
¹·(**d**　　　　　　　).

Haruka: Yeah, and there is a lot of ²·(**g**　　　　　　　), too. Oh no! Is that a
dead fish?!

Alex: I didn't realize the ³·(**p**　　　　　　　) in this area was so bad.
Someone should do something.

Haruka: Why don't we play ⁴·(**v**　　　　　　　) or throw the Frisbee instead?

Alex: Good idea. I'll take you to a ⁵·(**c**　　　　　　　) beach next time.

Listening Focus
🎧 DL 93　💿 CD2-28

■ t でつながる語句を聞き取る

　Unit 10 では t がのみこまれるように発音されて聞こえない場合について学習しました。単語の最後が t の音で終わり，次に母音で始まる語が続くときには別の注意が必要です。そのようなときは t が次の母音とリンキングして発音されます。

⇨ I can't wait to get in the water. では，
　　get の最後の t と in の最初の i がリンキングします。（※ wait の t はのみこまれます）
⇨ There is a lot of garbage. では，
　　lot の最後の t と，of の最初の o がリンキングします。

Practice
🎧 DL 94　💿 CD2-29

次の英文を聞き，下線部の t が次の母音とリンキングしていることを確認しましょう。確認したら，真似をして言ってみましょう。

1. What a waste of time!

2. Let it go! （※ it の t はのみこまれます）

3. Not at all.

READING PART

Find Out

DL 95　CD2-30

次のエッセイを読み，設問に答えましょう。

Save the Bees

Our friends, the bees, are in danger and need our help. As cities grow, there are fewer places for bees to live and find food. In the US, there were about 6 million honey bee hives in 1947. In 2008, there were only 2.4 million. Nowadays, farmers often use chemicals that are harmful for bees. This is a huge problem because a third of our food and 80% of our flowers need bees to grow. Many fruits, vegetables, and other foods would disappear without bees. Look online today and see what you can do for our friends.

Notes

hive「ミツバチの巣箱」 **chemical**「化学物質」

Check the Points

DL 96　CD2-31

音声を聞き，太字の語句のどちらが用いられているかを選びましょう。音声は２回繰り返されます。そして，完成した英文が本文の内容と合っていればT (True) を，合っていなければF (False) を選びましょう。

1. There were [**more** / **fewer**] bee hives in 1947 than in 2008. **[T / F]**

2. Most flowers [**need** / **don't need**] bees to grow. **[T / F]**

Reading Focus

■ **and がつなぐものを見抜く（並列1）**

次の英文の太字部分は，その文中にある and が並列につないでいるものです。

1. This park is **beautiful** and **clean**. （この公園は美しくてきれいです）
2. I read this book **at school** and **in the park**. （私はこの本を学校と公園で読みました）
3. **Haruka likes to play volleyball** and **Alex likes to throw the Frisbee**.
   （ハルカはバレーボールをするのが好きで，そしてアレックスはフリスビーをするのが好きです）

　and は，同じ種類のものを並列につなぎます。1 では語と語，2 では句と句，3 では節と節を並列につないでいます。and が何と何をつないでいるかを見極めることで，より理解が深まります。

Practice

次の英文は and を用いた文です。and によってつながれているものに下線を引きましょう。

1. Our friends, the bees, are in danger and need our help.

2. As cities grow, there are fewer places for bees to live and find food.

3. Look online today and see what you can do for our friends.

Practice More

日本語訳と頭文字のヒントを参考にして，and を使った英文を完成させましょう。

1. 絶対に飲酒して運転すべきではありません。

You should never **d**_____ and **d**_____.

2. 私の同僚のメグは私が信頼し，そして話をすることができる人です。

My co-worker, Meg, is the one I can **t**_____ and **t**_____
to.

3. 私は通りで飲み食いしていた彼女を見ました。

I saw her **e**＿＿＿＿＿＿＿ and **d**＿＿＿＿＿＿＿ on the street.

🔊 *Say What You Think*

DL 97　　CD2-32

日本語のヒントを参考にして次の文を読み，自らの意見に合うように表現を［　　］内から選びましょう。選んだら，その文を自分の意見として言ってみましょう。

1. I **[think / don't think]** bees in a big city are harmful to our lives.
(都市にいるハチは私たちの生活に有害だと思う／思わない)

2. I **[think / don't think]** farmers should stop using chemicals.
(農家の人々は化学薬品を使うことをやめるべきだと思う／思わない)

3. We **[need to / don't need to]** change our lifestyle to protect the environment.
(私たちは環境を守るために生活スタイルを変える必要がある／ない)

Unit 13
Economy & Industry

☑ **Listening Focus** ⇒ n でつながる語句を聞き取る
☑ **Reading Focus** ⇒ but や or がつなぐものを見抜く（並列2）

LISTENING PART

 **Listen In** 🎧 DL 98 💿 CD2-33

ユウタとアンナはランチタイムにコンビニから出てきたところです。上のイラストを見ながら，
アンナがユウタにした提案について聞き取ってみましょう。

 **Check the Points** 🎧 DL 99 💿 CD2-34

会話の内容に関する質問を音声で聞き，正しい答えを a 〜 c から選びましょう。

1. What does Anna eat for lunch?（アンナはお昼に何を食べる？）
   a. Homemade lunches   **b.** Take-away meals   **c.** Restaurant dishes

2. How much does Yuta spend for lunch every day?
   （ユウタは毎日どの程度お昼に使う？）
   a. ¥150   **b.** ¥600   **c.** ¥1,600

3. Who is probably going to make lunches for Yuta from tomorrow?
   （明日から誰がユウタにお昼を作ると思われる？）
   a. Yuta   **b.** Anna   **c.** His parent

61

⊖ *Check the Details*

もう一度会話を聞き，頭文字をヒントにして空所にあてはまる語を書き入れましょう。

Yuta: This store has the best lunches. Wait… You didn't buy anything?

Anna: Uh-uh. I always [1.](**b**   ) my lunches. It's so much cheaper that way.

Yuta: This isn't so [2.](**e**   )… I only spent about 600 yen.

Anna: 600 yen is a lot of money, Yuta! My lunch [3.](**c**   ) only about 150 yen to make.

Yuta: Really?! That's a big [4.](**d**   )! But I'm not good at cooking.

Anna: How about this? I'll bring your lunch, and you [5.](**p**   ) me 400 yen. It's a win-win!

Listening Focus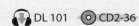

■ **n でつながる語句を聞き取る**

単語の最後が n で終わり，次に母音で始まる語が来るときには注意が必要です。n と母音がリンキングして「ナ」「ニ」「ヌ」「ネ」「ノ」のような音に聞こえます。

⇨ 600 yen is a lot of money, ... では，
yen の最後の n と，is の最初の i がリンキングして，「ニ」のように聞こえます。

自分で発音するときにも，そのように発音するようにしましょう。

Practice

次の英文を聞き，下線部の n が次の母音とリンキングしていることを確認しましょう。確認したら，真似をして言ってみましょう。

1. <u>When</u> is your birthday?

2 The <u>phone</u> is ringing!

3. I tried it <u>again</u> and again.

READING PART

 **Find Out**   🎧 DL 103 💿 CD2-38

次のエッセイを読み，設問に答えましょう。

YouTubers and Ad Revenue

Do you enjoy watching videos online but hate the advertisements? Sure, everyone does. Ads are annoying but necessary. They are how most websites,
5 such as YouTube, make money. Companies pay YouTube to show their commercials before, during, or after videos. You might not like these ads,
but here is the good news. If your videos are popular on YouTube, you can make
10 money, too. Famous YouTubers upload videos about things like games, news, or animals. One famous YouTuber made $7.4 million in 2019! Of course, not everyone makes that much, but a little extra cash is still nice.

Notes

advertisement (ad)「広告」 annoying「いらいらさせる，迷惑な」

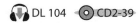 **Check the Points**   🎧 DL 104 💿 CD2-39

音声を聞き，太字の語句のどちらが用いられているかを選びましょう。音声は 2 回繰り返されます。そして，完成した英文が本文の内容と合っていれば T（True）を，合っていなければ F（False）を選びましょう。

1. Most online users find ads on websites to be [**interesting** / **annoying**].

[T / F]

2. [**Not every** / **Every**] YouTuber can make lots of money.   [T / F]

■ **but や or がつなぐものを見抜く（並列２）**
　次の英文の太字の部分は，but または or がつないでいる部分です。

1. She is **quiet** but **funny.**（彼女は物静かだけどおもしろいです）
2. When should I come, **today** or **tomorrow**?
　　（私が来るべきなのは今日ですか，それとも明日でしょうか）
3. **Tell her now** or **you never will**.
　　（彼女に今言いなさい。さもないとあなたは決して言わないでしょう）

　and と同様に but と or は同じ種類のものをつなぎます。1 では quiet と funny という形容詞，2 では today と tomorrow という副詞，3 では節と節をつないでいます。but と or が何と何をつないでいるかを見極めることで，より正確に理解できます。

Practice

次の英文は but または or を用いた文です。but または or によってつながれているものに下線を引きましょう。

1. Ads are annoying but necessary.

2. Companies pay YouTube to show their commercials before, during, or after videos.

3. You might not like these ads, but here is the good news.

⊘ Practice More

日本語訳と頭文字のヒントを参考にして，but または or を使った英文を完成させましょう。

1. 私の上司は私のオフィスに来たが，すぐに去りました。

My boss **c**_____ to my office, but he **l**_____ immediately.

2. 家にいたほうがいいですか。それとも外出すべきですか。

Should I stay **h**_____ or **g**_____ out?

3. 紙またはビニールのどちらの袋がいいですか。

Which kind of bag would you like, **p**＿＿＿＿＿＿ or **p**＿＿＿＿＿＿ ?

⊘ *Say What You Think*

🎧 DL 105 ◎ CD2-40

日本語のヒントを参考にして次の文を読み，自らの意見に合うように表現を［　　］内から選びましょう。選んだら，その文を自分の意見として言ってみましょう。

1. I [**like** / **don't like**] watching YouTube videos.
（私はユーチューブの動画を見るのが好きだ／好きではない）

2. I [**think** / **don't think**] being a YouTuber is a good way of making money.
（ユーチューバーはお金を稼ぐにはいい方法だと思う／思わない）

3. I [**think** / **don't think**] people will still be watching TV 20 years from now.
（今から 20 年後でも人々はテレビを観ていると思う／思わない）

Unit 14
Legal Issues

> ☑ **Listening Focus** ⇨ 話し手の気持ちを聞き取る
> ☑ **Reading Focus** ⇨ 文脈に合った意味を選ぶ（多義語）

LISTENING PART

 **Listen In** 🎧 DL 106 ◎ CD2-41

ミカコは偶然自転車に乗っていたゲイリーを見かけたことについて話しています。上のイラストを見ながら，自転車のルールについて聞き取ってみましょう。

 **Check the Points** 🎧 DL 107 ◎ CD2-42

会話の内容に関する質問を音声で聞き，正しい答えを a ～ c から選びましょう。

1. When did Mikako see Gary?（ミカコがゲイリーを見かけたのはいつ？）
   a. Last night   **b.** This morning   **c.** Tonight

2. What was Gary doing while riding his bicycle?
   （ゲイリーは自転車に乗っているとき何をしていた？）
   a. Listening to music   **b.** Singing   **c.** Eating

3. What will Gary do today?（ゲイリーは今日何をする？）
   a. Study law   **b.** Buy bicycle lights   **c.** Buy music CDs

⌾ *Check the Details*

🎧 DL 108 ◎ CD2-43

もう一度会話を聞き，頭文字をヒントにして空所にあてはまる語を書き入れましょう。

Mikako: Hey, Gary. I saw you riding your bicycle last night. I said hi, but you didn't ¹·(**n**   ).

Gary: Really? Sorry. Maybe I was listening to music. Where did you see me?

Mikako: Listening to music? Gary! You ²·(**c**   ) do that!

Gary: What? Why not? I do it all the time. It makes riding home more fun.

Mikako: It's ³·(**i**   ) in Japan! Also, you were riding without lights last night. It's not ⁴·(**a**   ) either!

Gary: Seriously? Okay. I'll go ⁵·(**b**   ) new lights today…

| Listening Focus /

🎧 DL 109 ◎ CD2-44

■ 話し手の気持ちを聞き取る

　同じ語句を用いた同じ文でも，話し手の気持ちによって聞こえ方が異なります。一般論として，他の条件が同じであれば，声の高さ（ピッチ）の上下動が大きいほど，強い感情を感じさせます。

⇨ Listening to music?
ここでは「音楽を聞いていたですって?! なんてことをしていたの！」という気持ちを込めて，ピッチのふれ幅が大きくなっています。

⇨ Gary! You can't do that!
ここでも，相手に対する非難・叱責の気持ちが，ピッチの大きな振れ幅に表れています。

| *Practice*

🎧 DL 110 ◎ CD2-45

次の英文を聞き，A よりも B のほうがピッチの上下動が大きく聞こえることを確認しましょう。確認したら，真似をして言ってみましょう。

1A. It's illegal in Japan.
1B. It's illegal in Japan!
2A. Where have you been? I have been looking for you.
2B. Where have you been?! I have been looking for you!

 *Find Out*

DL 111　CD2-46

次のエッセイを読み，設問に答えましょう。

Japan's Strict Bicycle Laws

Cycling around Japan is convenient, but you must pay attention to the rules. Japanese police might fine you for something that seems fine to you. For

5　example, don't listen to music or talk on the phone while riding. It's illegal. Riding a friend on the back of the bicycle is, too. If you are caught, you may have to pay up to 50,000 yen in fines. The penalty is the same for riding with no brakes or lights,

10　or with an umbrella. These fines aren't so light, so follow the rules and stay safe.

Notes

penalty「刑罰，罰則」　**brake**「ブレーキ」

Check the Points

DL 112　CD2-47

音声を聞き，太字の語句のどちらが用いられているかを選びましょう。音声は２回繰り返されます。そして，完成した英文が本文の内容と合っていれば T (True) を，合っていなければ F (False) を選びましょう。

1. It [**is** / **isn't**] convenient to ride bikes in Japan.　　　　　　　　**[T / F]**

2. Riding a bike with [**brakes** / **an umbrella**] is not allowed in Japan.

[T / F]

Reading Focus

■ 文脈に合った意味を選ぶ（多義語）

次の英文の太字部分は，複数の意味を持つ単語で多義語と言います。

1. We have to protect human **rights**.（私たちは人権を守らないといけません）

2. Turn **right** at the corner.（その角を右に曲がってください）

複数の意味がある単語でも，文脈で使われている意味は１つです。どの意味で使われているかは，前後の文脈や用いられている品詞から判断します。

Practice

次の英文では同一の単語が太字になっています。その単語の意味をそれぞれ（　）に書いてみましょう。

1. Japanese police might **fine** you for something that seems **fine** to you. 　（　　　　　　　）　　　　　　　（　　　　　　　　）

2. These fines aren't **so** light, **so** follow the rules and stay safe. 　（　　　　　　　）（　　　　　　　）

Practice More

次の英文の下線部には多義語が入ります。日本語訳と頭文字のヒントを参考にして，文を完成させましょう。

1. 私たちはこれを乗り越えられるでしょうが，強い意志がないといけません。

We **w**＿＿＿＿ get through this but we have to have a strong **w**＿＿＿＿.

2. 私はスポーツ科学を専攻しています。なぜならメジャーリーグに興味があるからです。

I **m**＿＿＿＿＿ in sports science because I am interested in the **M**＿＿＿＿＿ Leagues.

3. 以前，トムは車掌になるため研修を受けました。

Tom once **t**＿＿＿＿＿ himself to be a **t**＿＿＿＿＿ conductor.

⊘ *Say What You Think*

 DL 113 ◉ CD2-48

日本語のヒントを参考にして次の文を読み，自らの意見に合うように表現を［　　］内から選びましょう。選んだら，その文を自分の意見として言ってみましょう。

1. I [**think / don't think**] Japan's bicycle laws are too strict.
（日本の自転車の法律は厳しすぎると思う／思わない）

2. I [**think / don't think**] it is okay to ride a bicycle on rainy days.
（雨の日に自転車に乗ることは問題ないと思う／思わない）

3. I [**think / don't think**] it is okay to restrict the number of hours children play video games.
（子どもがゲームをする時間を規制するのはいいことだと思う／思わない）

Unit 15

Science & Technology

☑ **Listening Focus** ➡ 対比による強調を理解する
☑ **Reading Focus** ➡ 知らない単語の意味を推測する

LISTENING PART

Listen In
DL 114　CD2-49

ジョーイは新しく買ったスマートフォンについてアキコに話しています。上のイラストを見ながら，どんなスマホなのか聞き取ってみましょう。

Check the Points
DL 115　CD2-50

会話の内容に関する質問を音声で聞き，正しい答えを a～c から選びましょう。

1.　How does Joey feel about the new smartphone?
　　（ジョーイは新しいスマートフォンについてどう思っている？）
　　a. Excited　　**b.** Disappointed　　**c.** Worried

2.　How many cameras does the smartphone have?
　　（そのスマートフォンにはいくつカメラがある？）
　　a. One　　**b.** Two　　**c.** Five

3.　What is so special about Joey's smartphone?
　　（ジョーイのスマートフォンは何がすごい？）
　　a. Its color is cool.　　**b.** It is small.
　　c. It has two screens and takes clear pictures.

71

⊘ *Check the Details*

 DL 116 ⦿ CD2-51

もう一度会話を聞き，頭文字をヒントにして空所にあてはまる語を書き入れましょう。

Akiko: Whoa. Did you get a new phone again? You only used your last one for about a year!

Joey: I know, but this phone is ¹·(**a**   )! It's the best phone ever!

Akiko: You say that every time. What is so ²·(**s**   ) about this one?

Joey: It has two screens and ³·(**f**   ) cameras! The zoom is crazy too! I can almost see the future with it!

Akiko: Ha ha. That looks pretty cool! But are two screens really ⁴·(**n**   )?

Joey: Yes! Now I can watch videos and send ⁵·(**m**   ) at the same time.

Listening Focus

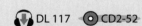 DL 117 ⦿ CD2-52

■ 対比による強調を理解する

Unit 1 で，名詞，動詞，形容詞，副詞などが文中では原則として強く発音されることを学習しました。そのほかにも，別のものと「対比」するときや「新しい情報」であることを伝えたいときには，その部分が強く発音されることがあります。

⇨ I know, but <u>this</u> phone is amazing!
この this は phone よりも強く発音されています。それは Akiko が言った your last one（= phone）つまり「前の」スマートフォンに対比して「この」スマートフォン，と強調したいためです。

Practice

 DL 118 ⦿ CD2-53

次の英文を聞き，強く聞こえる語に下線を引きましょう。確認したら，真似して言ってみましょう。

1. My father loves watching soccer games.

2. My father loves watching soccer games.

3. My father loves watching soccer games.

4. My father loves watching soccer games.

72

READING PART

 **Find Out**

DL 119 CD2-54

次のエッセイを読み，設問に答えましょう。

Smartphone Addiction

Are you addicted to your smartphone? You might be! Today's phones serve as our cameras, TVs, computers, and much more. However, spending too much time

5 on them can harm you. Every day, we see people browsing their phones while walking. This is very dangerous. Also, phones often distract people from work or study. At restaurants, too, people just look at their phones instead of having

10 conversations. In addition, staring at your phone for too long is bad for your eyes and posture. Are you spending too much time and energy on your smartphone? Maybe it's time to take a break from it.

 **Check the Points**

DL 120 CD2-55

音声を聞き，太字の語句のどちらが用いられているかを選びましょう。音声は2回繰り返されます。そして，完成した英文が本文の内容と合っていればT (True) を，合っていなければF (False) を選びましょう。

1. It is [**safe** / **dangerous**] to use our phones while walking.　　　　**[T / F]**

2. Spending a lot of time on your smartphone can be [**good** / **bad**] for you.

　　　　[T / F]

■ **知らない単語の意味を推測する**

次の英文の太字部分は，どのような意味だと思いますか。

1. My father is good at **sewing** a button on a sweater.
2. This painting describes the beauty of Mt. Fuji in a **vivid** manner.

　文中に知らない語が出て来ると，意味が理解できないことがあります。そのときは，まずその語の文の前後の意味を理解し，その意味を推測するようにしましょう。また，その語の品詞や文法的働きも考えましょう。1では，直後にある「セーターのボタン」から、sewing が動詞だとわかります。そこから「縫い合わせる」という意味を予測できます。2では、vivid は名詞の前にあるので形容詞だとわかります。「富士山の美しさを…と描写している」という意味となるので「どのように描写しているのか」を予測すればよいとわかります。

Practice

次の英文の太字部分の単語の品詞と意味を予想して（　　）に書いてみましょう。その後，辞書を用いて意味を確認しましょう。

1. However, spending too much time on them can **harm** you.
   　　　　　　（品詞：　　　　　　　　　）（意味：　　　　　　　　　）
2. Some people **browse** their phones while walking.
   　　　　　　（品詞：　　　　　　　　　）（意味：　　　　　　　　　）
3. In addition, looking at your phone for too long is bad for your eyes and **posture**.
   　　　　　　（品詞：　　　　　　　　　）（意味：　　　　　　　　　）

🔘 Practice More

次の英文の下線部には単語が入ります。日本語訳を参考にして，［　　］内にある名詞を適切な形に変えて文を完成させましょう。

1. 私たち家族はハワイを年一回訪れます。

   Our family makes a ＿＿＿＿＿＿ visit to Hawaii.　**[year]**

2. とても暑い日に運動するのは危険です。

It is _____ to exercise on a very hot day. **[risk]**

3. あなたのレベルを判定するためにこのクラス分けテストを受けてください。

Please take this _____ test so that we can identify your level.

[place]

 Say What You Think

DL 121 CD2-56

日本語のヒントを参考にして次の文を読み，自らの意見に合うように表現を [ ] 内から選びましょう。選んだら，その文を自分の意見として言ってみましょう。

1. I [**think / don't think**] it is okay to use a smartphone for many hours.
（長時間スマートフォンを使うことはいいと思う／思わない）

2. I [**think / don't think**] studying English with a smartphone is a great idea.
（スマートフォンを利用しての英語学習はいいことだと思う／思わない）

3. I [**think / don't think**] technology will make our lives better in the future.
（将来的にテクノロジーは私たちの生活をよりよくすると思う／思わない）

本書には音声 CD（別売）があります

AMBITIONS　Beginner

4 技能統合型で学ぶ英語コース：入門編

2021 年 1 月 20 日　初版第 1 刷発行
2024 年 2 月 20 日　初版第 5 刷発行

編著者　　VELC 研究会教材開発グループ
　　　　　靜　　哲　人
　　　　　望　月　正　道
　　　　　熊　澤　孝　昭

発行者　　福　岡　正　人
発行所　　株式会社　金　星　堂
（〒 101-0051）東京都千代田区神田神保町 3-21
Tel. (03) 3263-3828（営業部）
(03) 3263-3997（編集部）
Fax (03) 3263-0716
http://www.kinsei-do.co.jp

編集担当　西田碧　　　　　　　　　　Printed in Japan
印刷所・製本所／萩原印刷株式会社
ISBN978-4-7647-4119-5　　C1082